D1277765

Savannah
PERSPECTIVES

4880 Lower Valley Road, Atglen, Pennsylvania 19310

Matthew Propst

Dedication

For the 14 people killed on February 7, 2008 in the
sugar plant explosion in Port Wentworth, Georgia.

Thanks to:

Christ; Mother; B.J. Houck; Michelle Raab for the maps in Savannah Cemeteries; Brunson;
Atwell's Art & Frame; Creative Approach; Thomas Mott, *Savannah Getaways*; Wright
Square Cafe; Smooth; One Fish, Two Fish; The Barber Pole; Savannah Bee Company;
and Alexandra Farrugia

Schiffer Books are available at special discounts for bulk purchases for sales promotions or premiums. Special editions, including personalized covers, corporate imprints, and excerpts can be created in large quantities for special needs. For more information contact the publisher:

Published by Schiffer Publishing Ltd.
4880 Lower Valley Road
Atglen, PA 19310
Phone: (610) 593-1777; Fax: (610) 593-2002
E-mail: Info@schifferbooks.com

Copyright © 2010 by Matthew Propst
Library of Congress Control Number: 2009944170

For the largest selection of fine reference books on this and related subjects, please visit our web site at **www.schifferbooks.com**
We are always looking for people to write books on new and related subjects. If you have an idea for a book please contact us at the above address.

All rights reserved. No part of this work may be reproduced or used in any form or by any means—graphic, electronic, or mechanical, including photocopying or information storage and retrieval systems—without written permission from the publisher.
The scanning, uploading and distribution of this book or any part thereof via the Internet or via any other means without the permission of the publisher is illegal and punishable by law. Please purchase only authorized editions and do not participate in or encourage the electronic piracy of copyrighted materials.
"Schiffer," "Schiffer Publishing Ltd. & Design," and the "Design of pen and inkwell" are registered trademarks of Schiffer Publishing Ltd.

This book may be purchased from the publisher.
Include $5.00 for shipping.
Please try your bookstore first.
You may write for a free catalog.

Designed by Mark David Bowyer
Type set in Lucian BT / Zurich BT

ISBN: 978-0-7643-3460-3
Printed in China

In Europe, Schiffer books are distributed by
Bushwood Books
6 Marksbury Ave.
Kew Gardens
Surrey TW9 4JF England
Phone: 44 (0) 20 8392 8585; Fax: 44 (0) 20 8392 9876
E-mail: info@bushwoodbooks.co.uk
Website: www.bushwoodbooks.co.uk

Contents

Foreword

Savannah, Georgia, is unlike any other place in the world. It is a rich tapestry of history and modernity. The whispering fingers of the Spanish moss in the Live Oaks belie a vibrant southern town, founded in 1733. Savannah has and will continue to be a city of intrigue.

The intent of this book is to start the viewer on a visual journey that, it is hoped, will ultimately entice you to visit Savannah. The natural aesthetics of the place are captured in the instant, but, to truly appreciate its beauty and life, you must be here. When you come, you will want to make some photographs for yourself.

I have chosen to photograph six genres of life in Savannah for you to explore: its squares, historic places, the riverfront & parks, islands, colleges, and accommodations. There you will find traces of the city's memories dating back to its beginnings, and see how it continues to grow and change and create new memories with the passage of time.

1. Squares

In 1733, General James Oglethorpe led an expedition of 114 Englishmen, women, and children south from Charleston, in search of a viable site for a new settlement. He found what he was seeking on a high bluff on the western bank of the Savannah River, approximately 10 miles from the Atlantic Ocean. It was known as Yamacraw Bluff because the Yamacraw Native Americans lived in the area and with their blessing the site was obtained for the settlers.

Oglethorpe wrote the Trustees of the colony: "I chose this Situation for the Town upon high Ground, forty feet perpendicular above High Water Mark; the Soil dry and Sandy, the Water of the River Fresh...." [James Oglethorpe to the Trustees, February, 1733, in John Percival, *The Earl of Egmont Papers,* Phillips Collection, Hargett Rare Book and Manuscript Library, University of Georgia Libraries, 14200: 34-35].

It was the wish of the Oglethorpe and the Trustees to develop an egalitarian community in which all citizens had equal amounts of land. To this end, Oglethorpe developed a simple, yet highly sophisticated city plan. His design was a grid of square shaped units called "Wards," each having four sides of approximately 600 feet per side. At the center of each ward was a large, open space called a "Square." The four corners of each ward were called a "Tything." A tything consisted of ten house lots each, each 60 feet wide and 90 feet deep. These lots were reserved for the settlers' homes. On the east and west flanks of the squares were four larger lots known as the "Trustees Lots," which were reserved for public structures.

Johnson Square is located on Bull Street between Bryan & Congress. It was built in 1733 and named after Robert Johnson, Governor of South Carolina, who helped the infant colony, it was the first square. In the center of the square sits a monument to and the grave of General Nathaniel Greene. Overlooking the square is Christ Church, considered the "Mother Church of Georgia." Several major banks surround this square, the first of which was built in 1911.

Obviously, as the city grew new wards were created upon the original plan for the ward. All of the squares are approximately 200 feet from north to south, but vary from east to west from 100 to over 300 feet. Each square is bounded on the north by a narrow one-way street, running east to west and on the south by a narrow one-way street running west to east. Typically, a wider, two-way street intersects each side of a square and the wards are bounded on the north and south by wide east west through streets.

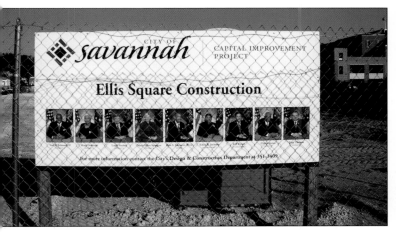

Also built in 1733, **Ellis Square**, on Barnard St. between Bryan & Congress, was named for Henry Ellis, second Royal Governor of Georgia. Sadly, this is one of Savannah's "Lost Squares," demolished when City Market was destroyed and replaced by a parking garage. The property will soon revert to city ownership and there are ongoing discussions among city officials about restoring it to some version of its original function. This is how it looks today.

Telfair Square, on Barnard Street between State & York, was also built in 1733 and originally called St. James Square and was re-named in 1883 for the Telfair family. The magnificent building, which houses the Telfair Museum, the oldest art museum in the South, and the Telfair Academy of Arts & Sciences, faces the square.

Nearby Ellis Square is Savannah's City Market, the historical center of commerce and now home to numerous art galleries, retailers, and restaurants.

Tomo-Chi-Chi rock at Wright Square honors the Native American who befriended and co-founded Savannah with John Oglethorpe. He was instrumental in the development of Savannah.

Wright Square, on Bull Street between State & York, was originally dubbed Percival Square in 1733, but was renamed in 1763 for Georgia's third and last Colonial Governor, Sir James Wright. For many years it has been colloquially known as Courthouse Square. A monument honors William Washington Gordon, an early Savannah mayor and founder of the Central Georgia Railroad. A large granite boulder marks the grave of Chief Tom chichi, who befriended Oglethorpe and his early band of settlers.

Washington Square, on Houston Street between Bryan & Congress, was laid out in 1790 and honors General George Washington. It is surrounded by beautiful homes with lovely architectural details.

Oglethorpe Square, on Abercorn Street between State & York, was laid out in 1742, and honors General Oglethorpe. Overlooking this square is the Owens-Thomas House, designed by William Jay and built 1816-1819. This lovely house is considered one of the finest examples of English Regency architecture in America.

Washington Square benches.

Franklin Square, on Montgomery Street at Congress (City Market), was established in 1790 to honor Benjamin Franklin. This square was nearly lost in the 1970s, which saw the demise of Elbert Square, but was ultimately restored to its original state. It is the site of First African Baptist Church.

Warren Square is on Habersham Street between Bryan & Congress. Laid out in 1791, it was named for the president of the Third Provincial Congress, General Joseph Warren, who was killed in the Battle of Bunker Hill. The Spencer House faces the square.

12

Columbia Square is at Habersham St. between York and State. Designed in 1799, at its center is a lovely cast iron fountain imported from the Wormsloe Plantation. Facing the square is the Davenport House, a fine example of Federal architecture. While every one of the squares is beautiful, this one is particularly lovely, shaded by four giant live oaks. Here, too, is the charming Victorian Kehoe House, built in 1892 by William Kehoe and now a restored inn.

Greene Square, on Houston Street between York & State, was established in 1799 and named for Revolutionary War General Nathaniel Greene, who is buried beneath the monument on Johnson Square.

Liberty Square is on Montgomery St. between State & York. Laid out in 1799, it was named for the Sons of Liberty, who fought for freedom against the British in the Revolutionary War. Another of the "Lost Square," the County Courthouse is now here, but in front of it burns the "Flame of Freedom." This is how it looks today.

The sign reads:

Savannah Civic Center

MAY
5   SAV TECH GRADUATION
6   PLATINUM AWARDS
9   AASU GRADUATION
21   GOLDEN AGE LUNCHEON
11-13 GA FUNERAL ASSO
13.   WALKER RECITAL

Welcome to the City of Savannah

Today, Elbert Square is home to the Savannah Civic Center.

Chippewa Square, on Bull St. between Perry & Hull, is named for the 1812 battle of Chippewa in Canada. An imposing statue of General James Oglethorpe is featured here. This is also the square made famous in modern days by the bench upon which Forest Gump sat in the movie of the same name.

Orleans Square is on north Barnard St. between Hull & Perry Streets. Laid out in 1815, it honors the War of 1812 Battle of New Orleans. The German Memorial Fountain at Orleans Square was built in 1989, and is quite lovely today.

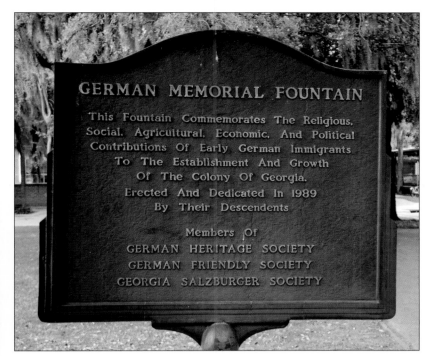

GERMAN MEMORIAL FOUNTAIN

This Fountain Commemorates The Religious,
Social, Agricultural, Economic, And Political
Contributions Of Early German Immigrants
To The Establishment And Growth
Of The Colony Of Georgia.
Erected And Dedicated In 1989
By Their Descendents

Members Of
GERMAN HERITAGE SOCIETY
GERMAN FRIENDLY SOCIETY
GEORGIA SALZBURGER SOCIETY

Lafayette Square, on Abercorn St. between Harris & Charlton, was laid out in 1837 and honors the Marquis de Lafayette. He visited Savannah in 1825 and spoke from the balcony of the Owens-Thomas House, which overlooks the square.

Owens-Thomas house at Lafayette Square.

Pulaski Square located at Barnard St. between Harris & Charlton. Laid out in 1837, it is named for Count Casimir Pulaski, the Revolutionary War hero from Poland, who sacrificed his life in the 1779 Siege of Savannah.

Reynolds Square is on Abercorn St. between Bryan & Congress. Honors Captain John Reynolds, Governor of Georgia in 1754. In 1969, the Methodists of Georgia erected a beautiful statue of their founder, John Wesley. Overlooking this square are the famous Pink House restaurant, the Lucas Theatre, and the lovely Planter's Inn.

The John Wesley statue
at Reynolds Square.

The Lucas Theater.

Crawford Square is on Houston St, between Hull & Perry. Laid out in 1841, it was named for William Harris Crawford, a Governor and United States Senator. It is the only remaining fenced square in the historic district. The structure covers a historic cistern holding water for fire fighting. There is also a basketball court in Crawford Square.

CISTERNS

MANY OF THE CITY'S SQUARES CONTAINED WATER CISTERNS TO AID IN FIREFIGHTING. THEY WERE KEPT FILLED WITH WATER AND WEEKLY REPORTS OF THE CONDITION AND WATER DEPTH WERE MADE TO THE CITY COUNCIL. THEIR DEPTH RANGED FROM 9 FEET 2 INCHES TO 15 FEET 5 INCHES. THEY WERE BUILT IN THE 1830'S AND 1840'S AND AMONG THEIR BUILDERS WERE AMOS SCUDDER AND CHARLES B. CLUSKEY.

Chatham Square is located on Barnard St.,
between Taylor & Gordon Streets. Laid out in 1847
it honors William Pitt, the Earl of Chatham.

Troup Square Habersham St. between Harris & Charlton. It is named for a former governor of Georgia, George Micheal Troup. Featured here is a dramatic armillary sphere, an astronomical model with solid rings, all circles of a single sphere, which is used to display relationship among celestial circles. The square was established in 1851.

Calhoun Square
is on Abercorn St. between Taylor and Gordon Laid out in 1851, it was named for South Carolina statesman, John C. Calhoun.

Monterey Square is also on Bull St. between Taylor & Gordon streets. Considered by many to be Savannah's most dramatic square, it is named for the capture of Monterey during the Mexican War in 1846 by American forces under the command of General Zachary Taylor. A monument of Count Casimir Pulaski is here.

Madison Square is located on Bull St. between Harris & Charlton. Laid out in 1837, it honors James Madison, fourth President of the United States. The square features a 15.5-foot statue of Sgt. William Jasper, killed in 1779 during the Siege of Savannah.

The Pulaski Monument at
Monterey Square.

Whitfield Square Is on Habersham St. between Gordon & Taylor streets. Laid out in 1851, it honors a Savannah minister, Rev. George Whitefield, the founder of the Bethesda Orphanage. It features a beautiful gazebo, often used, as the focal point for the square's numerous weddings.

2: Historic Sites / Architecture

Historic District Sign at Chatham Square.

Master-builder Isaiah Davenport completed this fine Federal-style in 1820 as his family residence home. Authentically restored, the house museum features original plasterwork, a cantilever staircase and furnishings true to the early 19th century. The site also features a courtyard garden that was originally a Bicentennial project of the Trustees' Garden Club and was later re-designed by noted horticulturist Penelope Hobhouse. Threatened with demolition in 1955, the saving of the Davenport House was the first effort of the Historic Savannah Foundation and the beginning of the historic preservation renaissance in this port city.

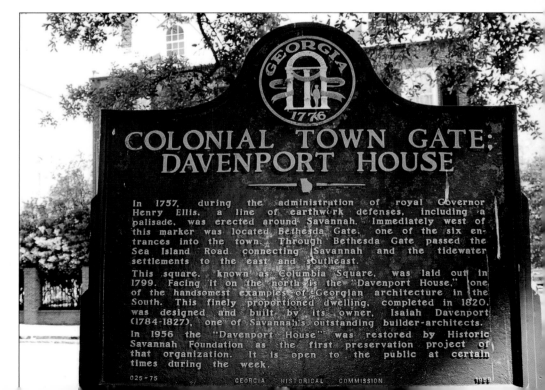

On April 11, 1862, defense strategy changed worldwide when Union rifled cannon first overcame a masonry fortification after only 30 hours of bombardment. Named for Revolutionary War hero, Count Casimir Pulaski, Fort Pulaski took some 18 years to build and was the first military assignment for a young second lieutenant fresh from West Point — Robert E. Lee. This remarkably intact example of 19th century military architecture, with its estimated 25 million bricks and 7.5-foot thick walls, is preserved for future generations by the National Park Service as a reminder of the elusiveness of invincibility. In 1996, 372,506 people visited the park.

Fort Pulaski weekend cannon firing demonstration.

Climb the ramparts of Fort Jackson and it is easy to see why this site was chosen to build a brick fort to protect Savannah. The year was 1808 and our relationship with Britain had worsened considerably over the past few years. Authorized by President Thomas Jefferson, Fort Jackson was built in Thunderbolt (now a section of Savannah) to protect the city from naval attack. Named for James Jackson, the fort is the oldest standing fort in Georgia. It was not the first fort to occupy the site, however. In 1776 Savannah residents built an earthen fort, which was destroyed by the construction of Fort Jackson. The fort was manned almost continuously during the first months of the War of 1812, when British privateers were setting fire to American sloops and schooners just off the coast of Georgia, and again near the end of the war when a British fleet under the command of Vice Admiral Alexander Cochrane was reportedly in the area . Residents of Savannah turned to old Fort Jackson for protection from the Union Navy during the War Between the States (Civil War). In addition to Fort Jackson, there were ironclads, (the Georgia and the Savannah), and a line of obstructions. Today the fort is owned and run by the Coastal Heritage Society.

Fort Jackson cannon overlooks the Savannah River.

The entrance to the Wormsloe Plantation ruins.

The writer and Savannahian, Flannery O'Connor's childhood home, downtown off Lafayette Square.

The Ralph Mark Gilbert Civil Rights Museum.

"TYRANTS FALL IN EVERY FOE
LIBERTY'S IN EVERY BLOW."

In memory of our Scottish forbears, whose
valor inspired these immortal lines by
Robert Burns, this marker is gratefully
dedicated by the Saint Andrew's Society of
Savannah, Georgia on its 250th Anniversary.
(1737 - 1987)
3 May 1987

Monument honoring Scottish forebearers on the median at the corner of Bull Street and Oglethrope Avenue.

The Roundhouse Museum.

Old Savannah Central railway car at the Roundhouse Museum.

The Jespon Center for the Arts is located in the Telfair Museum.

The First African Baptist Church, founded in 1777.

The magnificent dome of City Hall against some glorious clouds.

The International Seamen's House on Washington Square is a popular tourist point.

Christ Church, Anglican, considered the "Mother Church of Georgia."

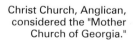

44

The Cotton Exchange was built in 1887 and is now home for the Savannah Chamber of Commerce. There is a restaurant on the lower level.

At The King-Tisdale Cottage, visitors may view antique African-American objects.

Signs in front of the birthplace of Juliette Gordon Low, founder of the Girl Scouts of America.

The Armstrong House, formerly the home of Armstrong Junior College, is at the top of Forsyth Park.

Savannah is very humid, seen here at the airport.

3. The Savannah River & Parks

The Savannah River at evening

Seagulls in flight over the Savannah River.

Tours of the Savannah River are offered nightly.

Savannah Riverfront, the Savannah River and the Talmadge Memorial Bridge.

Savannah River looking westward.

Fourth of July fireworks over the Savannah River, 2009

Savannah is on the Atlantic Intracoastal Waterway and has always been a port city.

Forsyth Park and Daffin Park are the two major parks maintained beautifully by the City of Savannah. James Oglethorpe established Forsyth Park as a backyard for the city resident.

Forsyth Park

The southern end of Forsyth Park, early morning.

Forsyth Park fountain, from a distance.

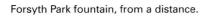

Forsyth Park fountain.

A statue honoring the Confederate dead at Forsyth Park.

The Fragrant Garden at Forsyth Park is home to numerous varieties of plants.

Inside the Fragrant Garden at Forsyth Park.

Every spring, Savannah College of Art & Design students paint the sidewalks of Forsyth Park with chalk.

The Farmers' Market at Forsyth Park has been going strong since 2009, and continues to provide Savannah with wholesome people and vegetables.

A hula dancer performs in Forsyth Park at night.

The Daffin Park fountain and sign.

4: Islands

Wilmington River, going to Wilmington Island. Wilmington Island, one of the Sea Islands in Chatham County, is just off the Atlantic coast, 10 miles East Southeast of Savannah, situated between two tributaries of the Savannah River. It is seven miles long and four miles wide. Much of the island is marshy and it is connected to the mainland by causeway.

Skidaway Island, another of the Sea Islands, is ten miles long and ten miles wide. Much of the land is marshy.

Early morning sun over the Wilmington River bridge from Savannah to Whitemarsh Island (pronounced 'Whitmarsh'). It has a total area of 6.6 square miles, 5.9 of which is land and 0.7 is water.

Three Whitemarsh Island palm trees.

Tybee Island, an incorporated town, is 15 miles east southeast of Savannah, at the mouth of the Savannah River. It is home to a lighthouse, Fort Pulaski, and Tybee Beach. The island is connected to the mainland by causeway.

The fishing pier at Tybee Beach.

A road sign on Tybee Island.

The Tybee Island Lighthouse is educational as well as beautiful, with a museum of the lighthouse's history on the grounds.

An antique tank on Tybee Island.

The view from atop the Tybee Island Lighthouse.

Isle of Hope

The Isle of Hope is said to be haunted.

Boats dock near the marina on the Isle of Hope.

A crab pot's point of view on the Isle of Hope.

Oatland Island has a zoo and education center. Of interest is a program that allows senior citizens to play with animals from the zoo.

5. Colleges

Youth is present in Savannah, juxtaposed against a glorious historical past. There are a number of colleges and universities in Savannah, including the Savannah College of Art and Design, Armstrong Atlantic State University (formerly Armstrong Junior College), and Savannah State University. These schools offer higher learning in a glorious environment.

The Savannah College of Art and Design administrative offices.

The Savannah College of Art and Design (SCAD) owns buildings throughout Savannah.

Bikes awaiting student riders at SCAD.

Armstrong Junior College sign.

6. Accommodations

There are many places to serve the tourists that visit Savannah. I have chosen to photograph a variety of restaurants and hotels with the weary traveler in mind.

Avia Hotel in downtown Savannah, 14 Barnard Street, 912-233-2116.

Clary's restaurant(s) in Savannah. This, the downtown location, at 404 Abercorn Street, 912-233-0402, is where several scenes are featured in the film "Midnight in The Garden of Good and Evil."

The Olde Pink House restaurant located at 23 Abercorn Street, 912-232-4286.

The Pirate's House Restaurante is at 20 E Broad Street, 912-233-5757.

The Kehoe House is located at 123 Habersham Street, 912-232-1020.

Mrs. Wilkes Dining Room at 107 W Jones Street, 912-233-5997, is a very popular eating site for both residents and tourists.

The Foley House Inn at 14 West Hull Street, 800-647-3708

About the Author

Matthew Propst grew up in Hickory, North Carolina. After completing his B.A. in English from the University of North Carolina at Greensboro, he received his MFA in Visual Art from Vermont College of Fine Arts.

He moved to Savannah, Georgia, and lives downtown. Matthew also photographs freelance for *The South* magazine and is in several galleries in the southeast. See more of his work at: www.mattpropst.com. Brunson is his dog that joins him often, everywhere.